Kids' Travel Guide
China

FlyingKids® Presents: Kids' Travel Guide China

Author: Jessica Wiseman, Shiela H. Leon
Editor: Carma Graber
Designer: Slavisa Zivkovic
Cover design: Francesca Guido Published by FlyingKids® Limited

Visit us @ www.theflyingkids.com

Contact us: leonardo@theflyingkids.com

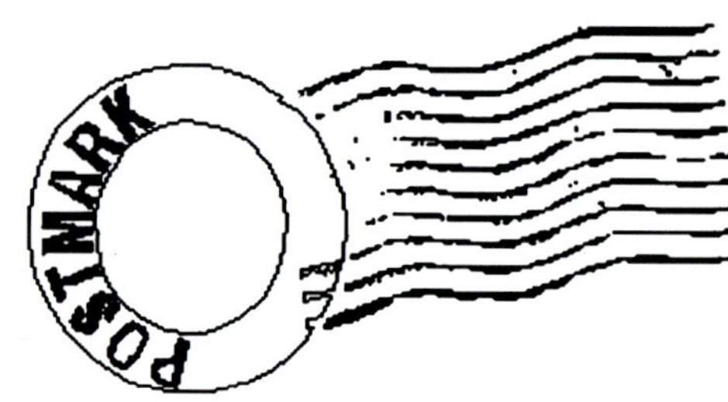

ISBN: 978-1-910994-57-3

Acknowledgments

All images are Shutterstock, except those mentioned below: Depositphotos images: 1bg-b, 26bc, 20bg, 21bg, 28bg, 29bg, 30bg-t, 31bg-b, 31bg-t, 34bg, 35bg, 38bg-t, 39t, 39bg-t, 41bg, 42bg. Others: 15l-LU JINRONG/Shutterstock.com, 15cr-LU JINRONG/Shutterstock.com, 16c-jack_photo/Shutterstock.com, 24t-Anton_Ivanov/Shutterstock.com, 27c-pieter/Shutterstock.com, 29t-Georg Denda [CC BY-SA 3.0] via Wikimedia Commons, 29b-Nuamfolio/Shutterstock.com, 30t-Nuamfolio/Shutterstock.com, 30b-Neale Cousland/.com, 38b-Aspen Photo/Shutterstock.com.

Key: t=top; b=bottom; l=left; r=right; c=center; m=main image; bg=background

Table of Contents

This is the only page for parents in this book ... 

Dear Parents,

If you bought this book, you're probably planning a family trip with your kids. You are spending a lot of time and money in the hopes that this family vacation will be pleasant and fun. You would like your children to learn a little about the country you visit—its geography, history, unique culture, traditions, and more. And you hope they will always remember the trip as a very special experience.

The reality is often quite different. Parents find themselves frustrated as they struggle to convince their kids to join a tour or visit a landmark, while the kids just want to stay in and watch TV. On the road, the children are glued to their mobile devices instead of enjoying the new sights and scenery—or they complain and constantly ask, "When are we going to get there?" Many parents are disappointed after they return home and discover that their kids don't remember much about the trip and the new things they learned.

That's exactly why *Kids' Travel Guide – China* was created.

With *Kids' Travel Guide – China*, young children become researchers and active participants in the trip. They learn fun facts about history and culture; they play games and take quizzes. This helps kids—and parents—enjoy the trip a lot more!

How does it work?

A family trip is fun. But difficulties can arise when children are not in their natural environment. *Kids' Travel Guide – China* takes this into account and supports children as they get ready for the trip, visit new places, learn new things, and finally, return home.

The *Kids' Travel Guide – China* does this by helping children to prepare for the trip and know what to expect. During the trip, kids will read relevant facts about China and get advice on how to adapt to new situations. *Kids' Travel Guide – China* includes puzzles, tasks to complete, useful tips, and other recommendations along the way. All of this encourages children to experiment, explore, and be more involved in the family's activities—as well as to learn new information and make memories throughout the trip. In addition, kids are asked to document and write about their experiences during the trip, so that when you return home, they will have a memoir that will be fun to look at and reread again and again.

Kids' Travel Guide – China offers general information about China, so it is useful regardless of the city or part of the country you plan to visit. It includes basic geography; flags, symbols, and coins; basic history; and colorful facts about the culture and customs of China.

Ready for a new experience?

Hi, Kids!

If you are reading this book, it means you are lucky—you are going to **China**!

You probably already know the places you will visit, and you may have noticed that your parents are getting ready for the journey. They have bought travel guides, looked for information on the Internet, and printed pages of information. They are talking to friends and people who have already visited China, in order to learn about it and know what to do, where to go, and when … But this book is not just another guidebook for your parents.

THIS BOOK IS FOR YOU ONLY—THE YOUNG TRAVELER.

So what is this book all about?

First and foremost, meet **Leonardo**, your very own personal guide on this trip. **Leonardo** has visited many places around the **world** (guess how he got there 😉), and he will be with you throughout the **book** and the **trip**. **Leonardo** will tell you all **about** the **places** you will visit—it is always good to learn a little bit about the country and its history beforehand. He will provide many **ideas**, **quizzes**, **tips**, and **other surprises**. **Leonardo** will accompany you while you are packing and leaving home. He will stay in the **hotel** with you (don't worry, it does not cost more money 😉)! And he will see the sights with you until you **return home**.

Have Fun!

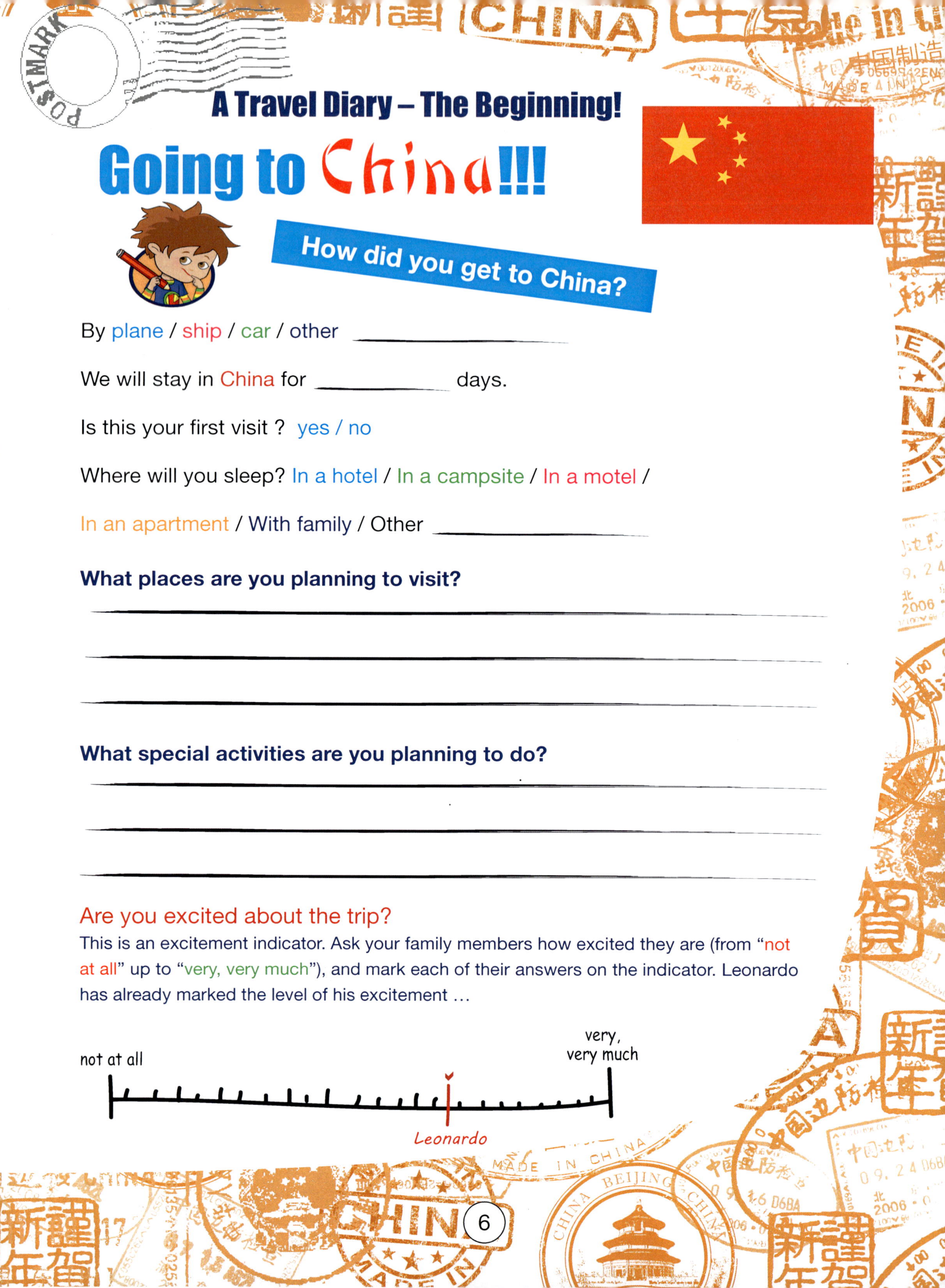

A Travel Diary – The Beginning!

Going to China!!!

How did you get to China?

By plane / ship / car / other ____________________

We will stay in China for ____________ days.

Is this your first visit ? yes / no

Where will you sleep? In a hotel / In a campsite / In a motel /

In an apartment / With family / Other ____________________

What places are you planning to visit?

____

____

____

What special activities are you planning to do?

____

____

____

Are you excited about the trip?

This is an excitement indicator. Ask your family members how excited they are (from "not at all" up to "very, very much"), and mark each of their answers on the indicator. Leonardo has already marked the level of his excitement …

not at all

very, very much

Leonardo

Who is traveling?

Write down the names of the family members traveling with you and their answers to the questions.

Paste a picture of your family.

Name: ________________

Age: ________

Have you visited China before? yes / no

What is the most exciting thing about your upcoming trip?

____

____

____

Name: ________________

Age: ________

Have you visited China before? yes / no

What is the most exciting thing about your upcoming trip?

____

____

____

Name: ________________

Age: ________

Have you visited China before? yes / no

What is the most exciting thing about your upcoming trip?

____

____

____

Name: ________________

Age: ________

Have you visited China before? yes / no

What is the most exciting thing about your upcoming trip?

____

____

____

Name: ________________

Age: ________

Have you visited China before? yes / no

What is the most exciting thing about your upcoming trip?

____

____

____

Preparations at home – DO NOT FORGET ...!

Mom or Dad will take care of packing clothes (how many pairs of pants, which comb to take ...). Leonardo will only tell you the stuff he thinks you might want to bring along on your trip to China.

Here's the Packing List Leonardo made for you. You can check off each item as you pack it:

- ☐ *Kids' Travel Guide* — ***China***—of course
- ☐ Comfortable walking shoes
- ☐ A raincoat (One that folds up is best—sometimes it rains without warning ...)
- ☐ A hat (and sunglasses, if you want)
- ☐ Pens and pencils
- ☐ Crayons and markers (It is always nice to color and paint.)
- ☐ A notebook or writing pad (You can use it for games or writing, or to draw or doodle in when you're bored ...)
- ☐ A book to read
- ☐ Your smartphone/tablet or camera
- ☐ ______________________________
- ☐ ______________________________

Pack your things in a small bag (or backpack).

You may also want to take these things:

Snacks, fruit, candy, and chewing gum. If you are flying, it can help a lot during **takeoff and landing**, when there's pressure in your ears.

Some games you can play **while sitting down:** electronic games, booklets of crossword puzzles, connect-the-numbers, etc.

Now let's see if you can find 12 items you should take on a trip in this word search puzzle:

- [ ] Leonardo
- [ ] walking shoes
- [ ] hat
- [ ] raincoat
- [ ] crayons
- [ ] book
- [ ] pencil
- [ ] camera
- [ ] snacks
- [x] fruit
- [ ] patience
- [ ] good mood

P	A	T	I	E	N	C	E	A	W	F	G
E	L	R	T	S	G	Y	J	W	A	T	O
Q	E	Y	U	Y	K	Z	K	M	L	W	O
H	O	S	N	A	S	N	Y	S	K	G	D
A	N	R	Z	C	P	E	N	C	I	L	M
C	A	M	E	R	A	A	W	G	N	E	O
R	R	A	I	N	C	O	A	T	G	Q	O
Y	D	S	G	I	R	K	Z	K	S	H	D
S	O	A	C	O	A	E	T	K	H	A	T
F	R	U	I	T	Y	Q	O	V	O	D	A
B	O	O	K	F	O	H	Z	K	E	R	T
T	K	Z	K	A	N	S	I	E	S	Y	U
O	V	I	E	S	S	N	A	C	K	S	P

Welcome to China!

China is a great country with an amazing history and a huge population. China is one of the world's most ancient civilizations. It has over 5,000 years of rich history. Today, more than one billion people live in the country!

In China, you can visit beautiful beaches and islands, hike through the tallest mountains in the world, and visit the sand dunes in the Gobi Desert. You can shop in China's beautiful cities, see towering skyscrapers, visit ancient temples, walk the Great Wall of China, and visit awesome palaces!

China is a very exciting place, and Leonardo can't wait to tell you all about this beautiful country! 🙂

Do you know what continent China is on?

____

Answer: Asia

How many words can you make from "Gobi Desert"?

beet

____

____

____

Did you know?
In ancient times, it was believed that China was the center of the universe. That's why the Chinese name for China is Zhong Guo, which means "Middle Kingdom."

Quizzes!

China is home to ...

1. Over one million people
2. Over ten thousand people
3. Just under five million people
4. Over one billion people

Answer: 4. Over one billion people

Where in the world is China?

Where is China on the map?

Can you point out China? Don't forget the islands!

Trace China's borders with your favorite color.

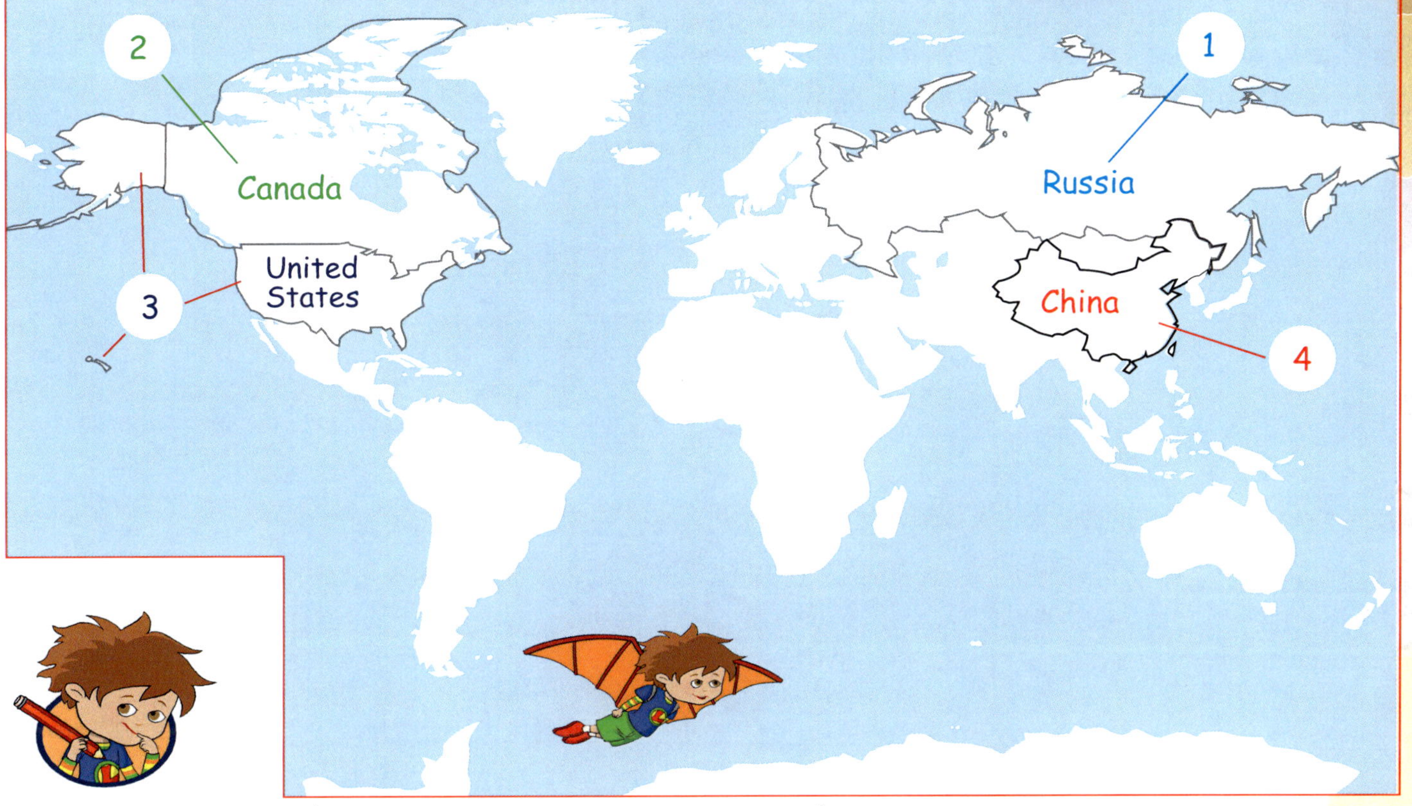

Leonardo wants to make a list of the four largest countries in the world. Can you check the map and help him?

1. ______________________

2. ______________________

3. ______________________

4. ______________________

Did you know?

China is the fourth largest country in the world. Russia is the largest country, Canada is second, and the United States is third. Even though those countries have more land than China, **China has more people. China has the biggest population of all the countries in the world!**

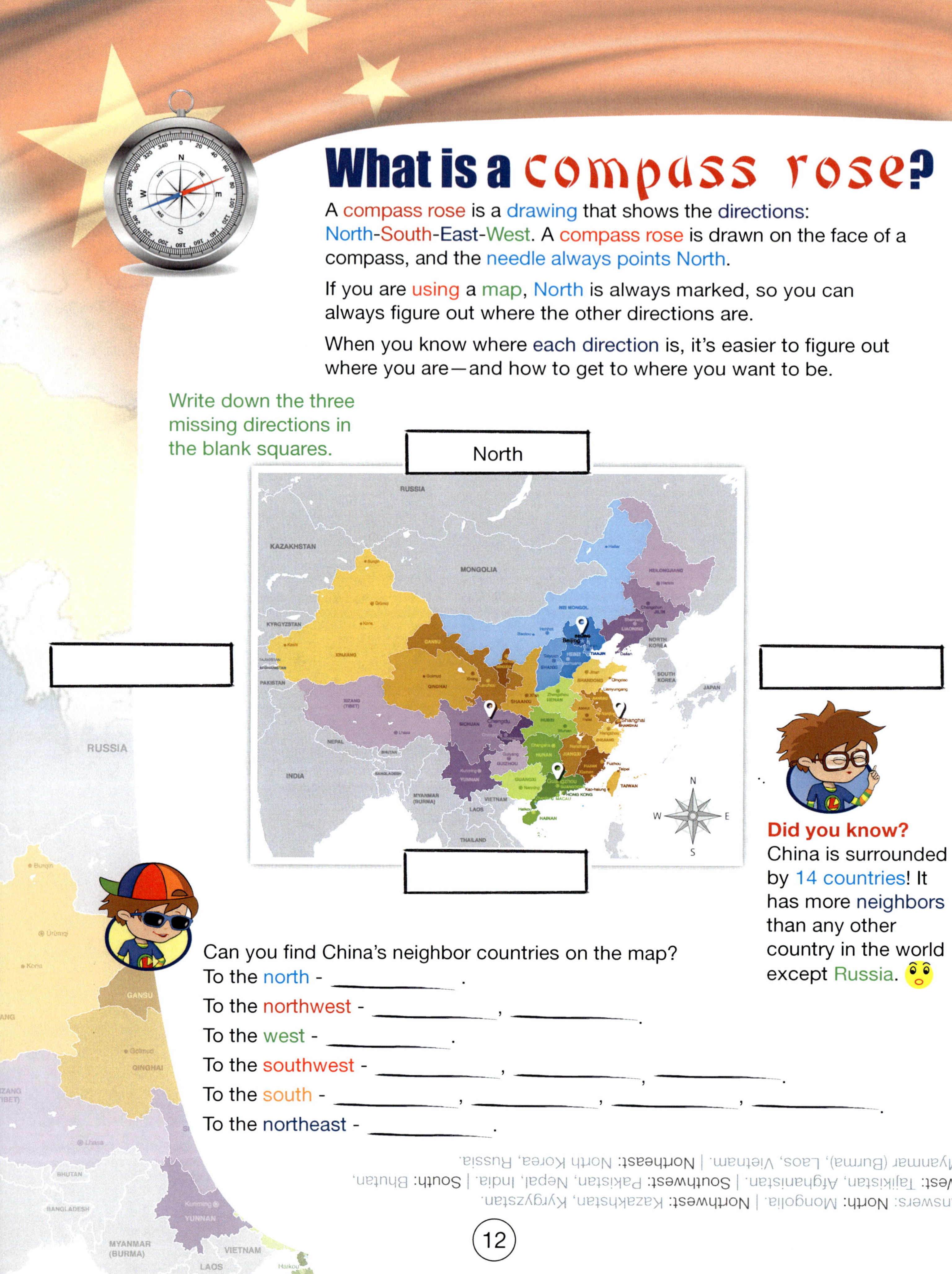

What is a compass rose?

A compass rose is a drawing that shows the directions: North-South-East-West. A compass rose is drawn on the face of a compass, and the needle always points North.

If you are using a map, North is always marked, so you can always figure out where the other directions are.

When you know where each direction is, it's easier to figure out where you are—and how to get to where you want to be.

Write down the three missing directions in the blank squares.

Did you know?
China is surrounded by 14 countries! It has more neighbors than any other country in the world except Russia.

Can you find China's neighbor countries on the map?

To the north - ____________.

To the northwest - ____________, ____________.

To the west - ____________.

To the southwest - ____________, ____________, ____________.

To the south - ____________, ____________, ____________, ____________.

To the northeast - ____________.

Answers: North: Mongolia. | Northwest: Kazakhstan, Kyrgyzstan. West: Tajikistan, Afghanistan. | Southwest: Pakistan, Nepal, India. | South: Bhutan, Myanmar (Burma), Laos, Vietnam. | Northeast: North Korea, Russia.

All about borders

Did you know?

Borders were created so we can tell where one country ends and another begins. Borders are lines drawn on maps. You won't see a line on the ground showing you where China begins and Mongolia ends!—but there are different types of borders that you can see. Sometimes countries are separated by natural borders like rivers or mountains. In other places, people put up a fence or a gate to mark a border. In China, many tall mountains form a natural border to the west. To the north, there was no natural border, so the ***Great Wall of China*** was built to protect the country.

To the east, China is bordered by seas. Can you find their names?

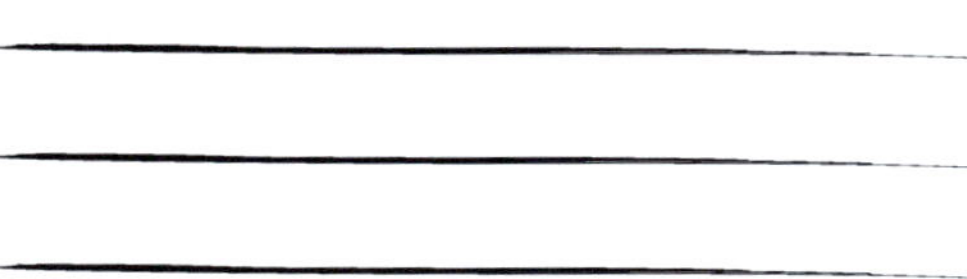

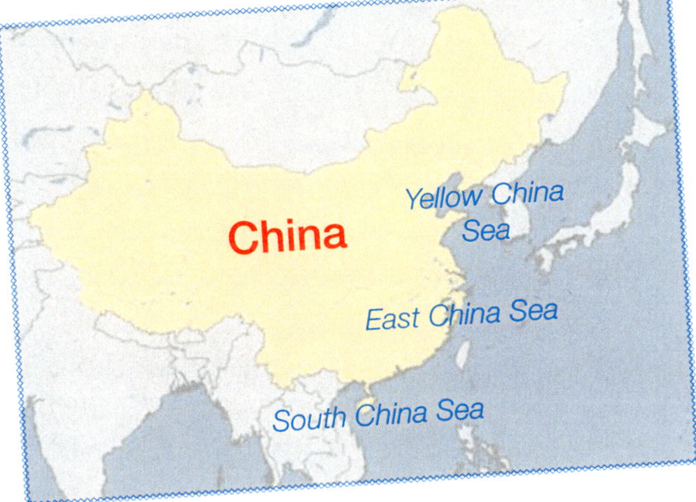

Quizzes!

You are about to visit beautiful China! Can you find eight Chinese cities in the word search puzzle?

- ☑ Shanghai
- ☐ Beijing
- ☐ Guangzhou
- ☐ Shenzhen
- ☐ Tianjin
- ☐ Dongguan
- ☐ Hangzhou
- ☐ Chengdu

D	Q	J	Y	H	Z	R	B	J	U	F	Q
O	O	E	U	J	I	E	N	B	O	N	A
U	H	N	M	K	I	Y	I	P	H	I	V
H	D	D	G	J	M	A	O	H	Z	X	G
N	L	G	I	G	H	N	T	A	G	Y	O
G	Q	N	N	G	U	Q	S	N	N	Y	B
V	G	D	N	E	L	A	X	G	A	I	T
H	J	A	D	G	H	I	N	Z	U	E	T
T	H	E	I	Q	W	C	C	H	G	P	C
S	N	I	J	N	A	I	T	O	U	I	X
S	H	E	N	Z	H	E	N	U	K	A	E
E	K	L	W	Z	P	E	V	O	R	T	Y

Answers: Yellow China Sea, East China Sea, South China Sea

Beaches, deserts, and mountains ... hot and cold weather!

How big is China? It's 9,596,960 square kilometers (3,705,405 square miles). Because it's so large, it has a lot of different types of land. It is mostly made up of mountains and high plateaus, but it also has sandy deserts, open plains, dense forests, hilly areas, and fertile river deltas. And then there are the beautiful beaches of the three seas on China's eastern border.

China has several different climates. In the south, the weather is very tropical—warm and humid. In the north, it is subarctic—meaning it can get very cold! You can go snow skiing in parts of China, while at the same time, it's hot and dry in the desert!

Quizzes!

1. Can you go to the beach in China? Yes / No
2. Is it always warm everywhere in China? Yes / No
3. Does China have any forests? Yes / No
4. Could you play in the snow in parts of China? Yes / No

Answers: 1. Yes, 2. No, 3. Yes, 4. Yes

Let's have a look at China's main cities ...

China's capital city: Beijing

Beijing, China's bright and beautiful capital city, is home to over 19 million people.

Beijing is one of the four ancient cities of China. It is home to Dragon Bone Hill, where ancient human fossils have been discovered.

Because Beijing is such an old city, it has been known by many other names throughout its history. Over the past 3,000 years, it has been known as Peking, Jicheng, Yanjing, Guangyang, Fanyang, Jixian, Youzhou, and more!

Beijing is home to many historic places, monuments, museums, temples, palaces, tombs, pagodas, and gardens. You can visit a popular part of the Great Wall of China here, called **Badaling**.

Did you know?
Beijing means "Northern Capital." The Chinese characters for Beijing are:北 (north) and 京 (capital).

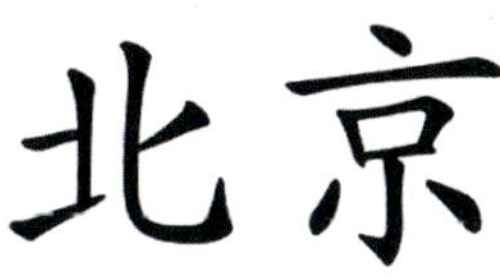

北京

The Chinese characters for Beijing

Did You Know?
To build the **Great Wall of China** today, it would cost 293 billion British pounds, or 360 billion American dollars, or 249 trillion Chinese yuan!

Shanghai—China's largest city

With 22 million people, Shanghai is China's largest city. It is also the wealthiest city in China. The city has a very large and busy port that receives and ships many goods. Shanghai is the largest trade center in China, so it is very important to China's economy.

Shanghai has two very large airports. (*Will you be flying in to Shanghai?*) And it has the **world's fastest train**. It's called the Maglev.

Shanghai is located on the Yangtze River delta in the center of China's eastern coast.

Can you help Leonardo connect the dots and color the Buddha statue?

Did you know?
The Yangtze River is the **third longest river in the world.**

You'll find the Jade Buddha Temple in Shanghai. It has beautiful jade statues and an amazing garden—and it's home to 70 working monks.

You can also see the Zhujiajiao water town in Shanghai. It's an ancient town with beautiful old bridges over waterways and Chinese-style homes from long ago.

Guangzhou—
where things get made

Millions of people from the Chinese countryside travel to Guangzhou to work in its many factories. Guangzhou is a huge manufacturing center for China and for the world. Toys, clothes, electronics, and other plastic goods are made here and shipped all over the world.

About 11 million people live in Guangzhou, making it China's third largest city. How many people live in your city? ____________

While much of Guangzhou is crowded, there are fun things to see and visit, including the Chimelong Safari Park, Chimelong Circus, and the Chimelong Water Park. The Canton Tower is Asia's second tallest tower. It has a special observatory where you can see as far away as Hong Kong.

Circle the items that could have been made in Guangzhou's factories.

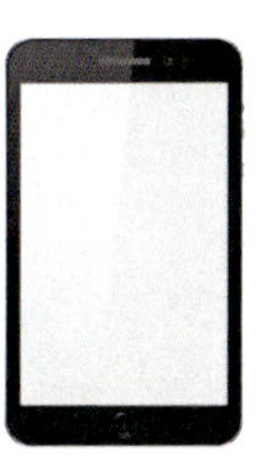

Answers: All of these items could have been made in Guangzhou!

Chengdu—giant pandas!

Most of China's large cities are situated in East China, near the Pacific coast. Chengdu is the exception! It's in west central China, in the Sichuan Basin.

Over seven million people live in Chengdu. It enjoys a more relaxed pace than the bigger eastern cities.

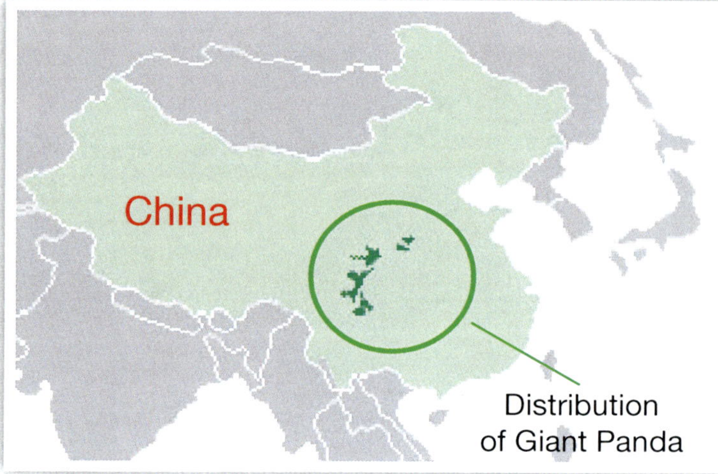

Chengdu is best known for its giant panda bears! Leonardo suggests you visit the Giant Panda Breeding and Research Base in Chengdu. You can see baby pandas, and even hold and feed them!

Pandas are endangered because humans have cut down so many of the bamboo forests pandas need to survive. "Endangered" means an animal is at risk for becoming extinct.

Do you know any other endangered species? Write down what you know. How do you think we can help them?

____

____

____

____

Where do pandas live?

They live in bamboo forests on high, humid mountain slopes. Pandas love to eat the shoots and stems of the bamboo plant. They can eat almost 40 kilograms (88 pounds) of bamboo per day!

How big are pandas?

Giant pandas are about the same size as human adults. Pandas average 1.5–1.8 meters (5–6 feet) long, from nose to tail. They weigh around 68–100 kilograms (about 150–220 pounds). Newborn pandas are very small and weigh only about 100 grams (or 3-1/2 ounces)!

Flags and symbols

This is China's flag.

It has a red background, with five yellow stars.

One star is larger and stands for China and the Communist Party of China (their system of government). The four smaller stars represent the four social classes or the different minorities that make up China. The background is red to represent the bloodshed of those who died during China's civil war and revolution and to honor them.

China's flag

This is the Coat of Arms of China.

It is the national seal. It shows the entrance gate to the Forbidden City in Beijing. The five stars above it are the same stars from the flag. The largest one stands for the government and the Communist Party, and the four smaller stars represent the people.

Forming a circle around the edges are sheaves of wheat and rice. These represent the agricultural revolution. The cogwheel at the bottom of the circle represents the factory workers of China.

Coat of Arms of China

Draw a line to the picture of China's other symbols.

Giant Panda (National animal)

Red-Crowned Crane (National bird)

Ginkgo (National tree)

Ping-Pong (National sport)

Buying things in China ...
Paper money and coins

The type of money a country uses is called its "currency." Chinese currency is officially called the renminbi (or RMB). Renminbi means "the people's currency." The actual Chinese money is called the **yuan**. If you are confused, don't worry. Renminbi and yuan are both recognized to mean money.

The Chinese coins are:

1 yuan

Jiao: 1/10 yuan
(or one Chinese dime)

Fen: 1/10 jiao
(or one Chinese penny)

Chinese paper money, or yuan notes, has six different bills: 1-, 5-, 10-, 20-, 50-, and 100-yuan. The paper money comes in different sizes and colors, but all the bills have a picture of Chairman Mao. The back of each bill shows a famous place in China.

Can you draw the sign for the Chinese yuan?

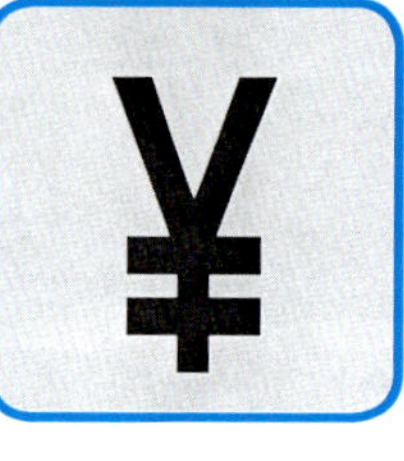

Did you know?
Chinese coins weren't always round. Some of China's first money was made of carved shell or bone. The first metal coins were shaped like a spade. Later, coins were made in the shape of knives! China's first round coins had round or square holes in the middle.

China's ancient history—dynasties!

Leonardo wants to take you on a quick trip through China's history. He made this list of the 10 dynasties that ruled China. (A dynasty is when the same family stays in power for a long period of time.) China's dynasties started in 2070 BC ("before Christ") and lasted till 1912 AD ("after Christ").

2070 BC	**Xia Dynasty:** The **earliest**-known dynasty was the first to work with **bronze**.
1570 BC	**Shang Dynasty:** Thirty emperors ruled over a period of 554 years.
1045 BC	**Zhou Dynasty:** The **longest** dynasty lasted 790 years and had 37 emperors.
221 BC	**Qin Dynasty: The Great Wall of China** was started.
206 BC	**Han Dynasty:** Papermaking was invented during this 400-year dynasty.
618 AD	**Tang Dynasty:** Known as the **Golden Age** of ancient China for its poetry and art.
907 AD	**Five Dynasties:** Lasting 53 years, this period includes **five dynasties**.
960 AD	**Song Dynasty:** China was reunited, and the **compass** was invented.
1368 AD	**Ming Dynasty: Finished** the **Great Wall of China** and built the **Forbidden City**.
1644 AD	**Qing Dynasty: The last** of China's ancient dynasties lasted until 1912.

Leonardo forgot some important facts about Chinese history. Can you help him?

1. Which dynasty was considered the Golden Age of China?
- a) Qing Dynasty
- b) Tang Dynasty
- c) Xia Dynasty

2. Which dynasty was the last one?
- a) Han Dynasty
- b) Six Dynasty
- c) Qing Dynasty

3. Which dynasty included more than one ruling family?
- a) Sui Dynasty
- b) Five Dynasties
- c) Six Dynasties

4. During which dynasty was the Great Wall of China completed?
- a) Han Dynasty
- b) Qin Dynasty
- c) Ming Dynasty

5. During which dynasty was the compass invented?
- a) Tang Dynasty
- b) Song Dynasty
- c) Yuan Dynasty

6. Which dynasty was the longest reigning dynasty?
- a) Zhou Dynasty
- b) Song Dynasty
- c) Yuan Dynasty

Answers: 1. b) Tang Dynasty; 2. c) Qing Dynasty; 3. b) Five Dynasties; 4. c) Ming Dynasty; 5. b) Song Dynasty; 6. a) Zhou Dynasty.

Modern China

China's last dynasty—the Qing Dynasty—ended when the Republic of China was formed in 1912. Then in 1949, the Communist Party seized control of the government and all the businesses in China. Their leader, Mao Zedong (mou dzeh-doong) established the People's Republic of China.

Mao started what he called the Cultural Revolution, and **millions of people were put in prison or killed**. When Mao died in 1976, China was very poor, and most people were uneducated.

In the late 1970s and early 1980s, new leaders began to make things better, and China became the world's fastest-growing economy. It's now the ***world's biggest trader of goods***. And it has the second highest number of billionaires in the world! Regular Chinese people are becoming more wealthy too!

China's relationships with other nations have been better since Mao died, but some countries still want China to give its people more freedom. Even now, people can be put in jail for saying bad things about the Chinese government.

Did you know?
From 1979 to 2015, kids born in China could **not have brothers or sisters**! It was against the law for most families to **have more than one child**. This law is now ending.

What is the government like in your country? Write what you know about it.

____

____

Circle Yes or No:

1. Mao Zedong started the Cultural Revolution. YES or NO

2. It is still illegal for parents to have more than one child in China. YES or NO

Answers: 1.)Yes; 2.) No

China's famous landmarks:
The Great Wall of China

Do you remember when Leonardo told you about China's dynasties a few pages back? The first emperor of the Qin Dynasty was named **Emperor Qin Shi Huang**. He united China as one country, and he began to build what would become the Great Wall of China.

After **Emperor Qin**, many emperors put people to work on the wall. The workers were usually criminals or enemies who had been captured—and they were treated like slaves. Many workers died from accidents, diseases, or exhaustion.

Fun Facts about the Great Wall of China

- If you tried to walk from the beginning of the wall to the end, it would take you more than a year and a half! That's because it's 6,300 kilometers (3,915 miles) long! That's about the **distance between New York City and Stockholm, Sweden**!
- The wall is **more than just a big fence**. It has lookouts and signal towers, plus places for soldiers to sleep.
- At first, they built the wall out of packed dirt and rocks. Later, the **Ming Dynasty** finished the wall using bricks.
- The wall took 1,700 years to finish … **Wow**! 

Can you guess the answer?

1. Some people think astronauts can see the Great Wall of China from the moon. Do you think that's true? Circle **TRUE** or **FALSE**.

2. Some people think the slaves who died while building the wall have a special gravesite. Do you think that's true? Circle **TRUE** or **FALSE**.

Answers: 1.) False! Humans can't see the wall from space without special tools. 2.) False! They were buried under the wall!

China's landmarks: Terracotta Army

Emperor Qin, who united China and began the **Great Wall of China**, wanted to live forever! When he couldn't find a way to become immortal, he built himself a giant tomb. It is the **largest single tomb built for a leader in the history of the world**! Qin also built an army of clay soldiers to accompany him into the next life and protect him. He probably used about 700,000 workers to build over **8,000 life-sized statues of soldiers**. There were also 150 life-sized cavalry horses, 520 regular horses, and 130 chariots made of clay. They were all buried with the emperor.

Did you know?
The statues of the horses had saddles, which proves that **saddles had been invented by 221 BC**!

China's landmarks: Forbidden City

The Forbidden City is a grand palace in China's capital, Beijing. It was used by the emperors of China during the Ming and Qing **Dynasties**. More than one million workers built it between 1406 and 1420. They used specially made golden bricks—along with marble and wood from the very rare zhennan tree (**one of the most expensive kinds of wood in the world**)! The Forbidden City is now a museum you can visit. It has almost 9,999 rooms—and is almost 140,000 square meters (1.5 million square feet). Imagine how long it would take to clean!

China's landmarks:

The Ming Tombs are located near Beijing at the foot of the Tianshou Mountains. Leonardo thinks the tombs look almost like palaces! Thirteen of the 16 Ming Dynasty emperors (and their wives) are buried here.
To visit the tombs, you walk down a wide avenue called the **Sacred Way**. It's guarded by huge stone statues of animals and humans that tower above you. Take a picture with your favorite statue!

Did you know?
The first and largest tomb is the Changling Tomb. The Dingling Tomb is the third largest. To explore its system of passages and chambers, you have to go deep below ground.

Quizzes!

Can you find China's famous landmarks?

- [x] Terracotta Army
- [ ] Ming Tombs
- [ ] Grand Canal
- [ ] Great Wall of China
- [ ] Forbidden City
- [ ] The Bund
- [ ] Potala Palace
- [ ] Temple of Heaven
- [ ] Summer Palace
- [ ] Jiuzhaigou

T	W	N	D	Z	C	Q	U	O	C	W	P	Q	Q	F	A	Y	U
T	E	R	R	A	C	O	T	T	A	A	R	M	Y	N	F	P	O
L	W	M	J	B	M	D	D	E	S	E	J	U	I	I	O	Q	G
N	A	B	P	P	T	H	E	B	U	N	D	H	S	T	R	U	I
W	R	N	J	L	G	O	M	Q	Q	M	C	X	A	O	B	B	A
S	W	Z	A	F	E	O	A	T	D	F	P	L	V	W	I	N	H
P	S	A	Y	C	T	O	W	K	O	P	A	O	A	A	D	T	Z
J	H	R	T	G	D	Q	F	L	R	P	D	W	B	G	D	W	U
E	T	W	N	L	T	N	L	H	A	P	T	S	H	A	E	T	I
A	Q	I	U	R	V	A	A	L	E	R	E	T	F	Y	N	I	J
O	M	H	Q	Z	W	A	A	R	Z	A	K	F	V	D	C	M	T
Z	O	U	G	T	O	C	V	H	G	Z	V	W	V	W	I	R	S
W	F	R	A	B	E	X	X	K	V	D	A	E	W	W	T	Q	W
T	M	E	M	S	H	U	Z	F	X	S	E	V	N	R	Y	A	R
I	R	E	C	A	L	A	P	R	E	M	M	U	S	I	P	N	C
G	I	D	R	Y	H	T	G	X	R	K	O	R	M	U	I	T	Q
J	E	N	H	W	V	T	J	K	C	J	O	A	W	G	L	B	Z
O	W	A	Q	D	P	S	I	G	E	M	Q	M	C	Y	T	A	F

China's inventions

China is famous for its many inventions that changed the world. Can you guess which of the things on this page they didn't invent?

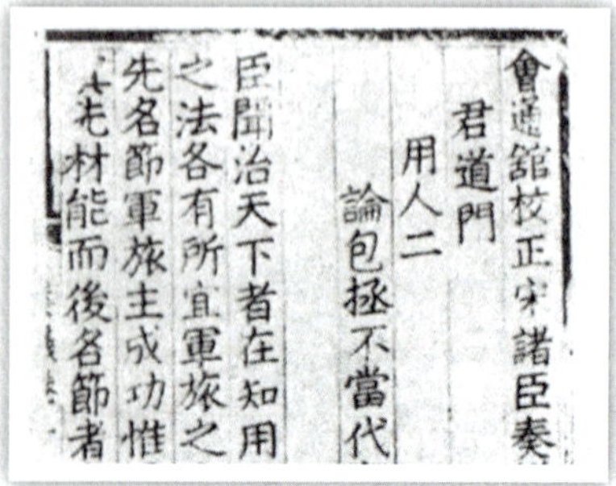
會通館校正宋諸臣奏
君道門
用人二
論包拯不當代
臣聞治天下者在知用
之法各有所宜軍旅之
先名節軍旅主成功惟
材能而後名節者

Movable type

Paper

Rocket launcher

Gunpowder

Compass

Toilet Paper

Silk

Kite

Umbrella

Surprise! The Chinese invented ALL of these and more! They are responsible for giving us hot air balloons, matches, the abacus, porcelain, the wheelbarrow, cast iron, stirrups, seismographs for measuring earthquakes, rotating fans, tea, alcohol, and much, much more!

Culture and customs

The Chinese people have many wonderful festivals, but the Chinese New Year (also called Lunar New Year) is China's biggest holiday. It has been celebrated for over 4,000 years!

China's factories and businesses close down for the New Year. Millions of people travel to their childhood homes to celebrate with their families. Children receive "lucky red envelopes" containing money from family and friends. They look forward to setting off firecrackers and watching parades with dragon and lion dances!

The Chinese people also love music and operas. The costumes are very elaborate and beautiful! Some operas include acrobatics, fire-breathing, or juggling tricks.

Which kind of character would you like to be? Color your own mask!

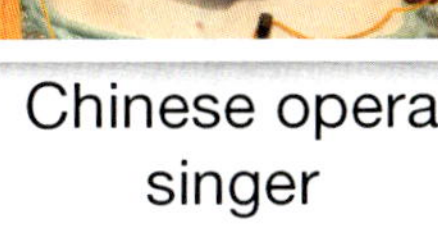
Chinese opera singer

Did you know?

Chinese opera singers wear color-coded masks. Once you know the code, you can tell who the characters are and how they might act. Circle the one you would like to wear.

Yellow mask: ambitious
White mask: evil
Black mask: fierce
Green mask: violent
Red mask: brave

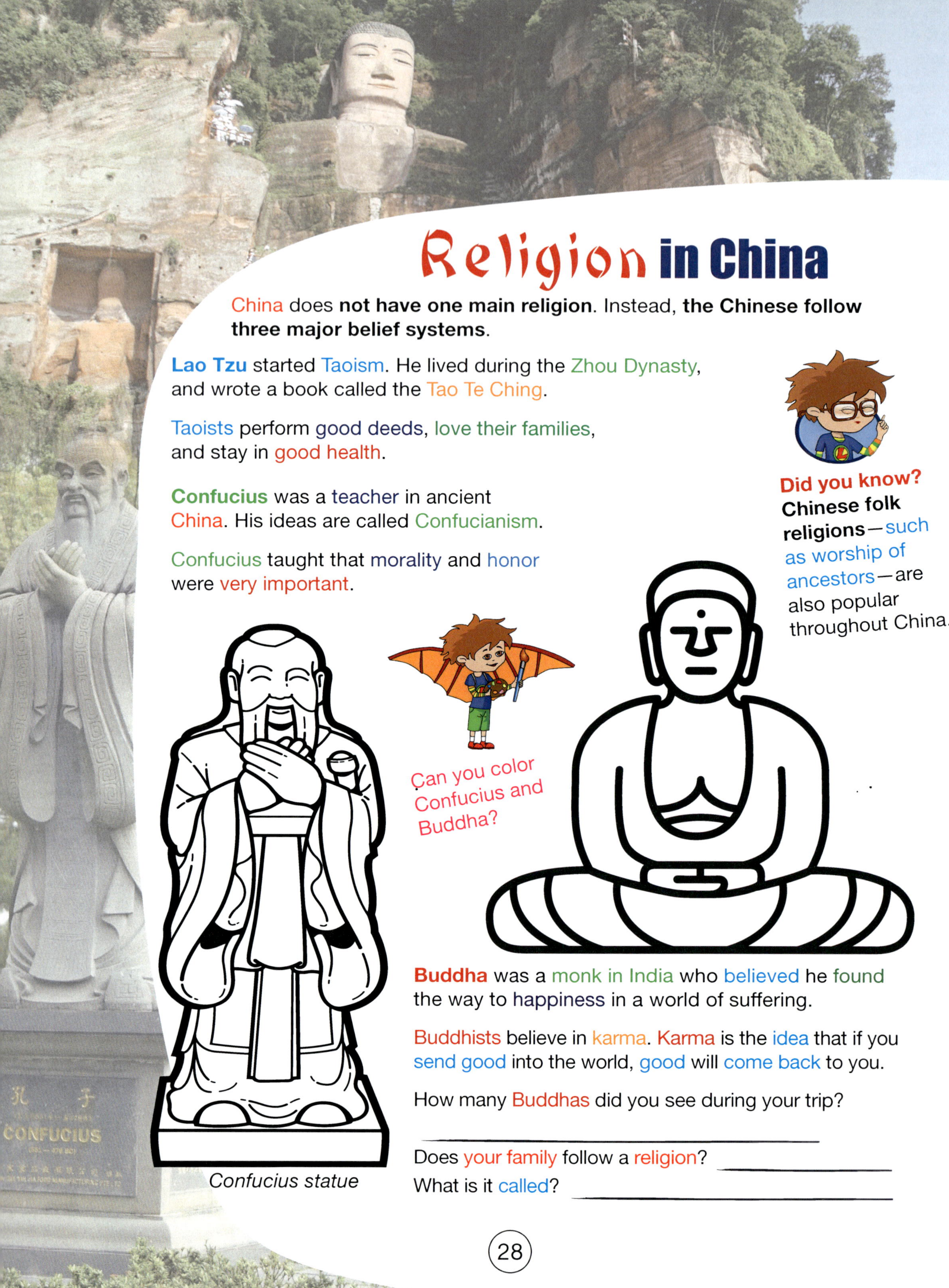

Religion in China

China does **not have one main religion**. Instead, **the Chinese follow three major belief systems**.

Lao Tzu started Taoism. He lived during the Zhou Dynasty, and wrote a book called the Tao Te Ching.

Taoists perform good deeds, love their families, and stay in good health.

Confucius was a teacher in ancient China. His ideas are called Confucianism.

Confucius taught that morality and honor were very important.

Did you know?
Chinese folk religions—such as worship of ancestors—are also popular throughout China.

Confucius statue

Buddha was a monk in India who believed he found the way to happiness in a world of suffering.

Buddhists believe in karma. Karma is the idea that if you send good into the world, good will come back to you.

How many Buddhas did you see during your trip?

____

Does your family follow a religion? ____________

What is it called? __________________

Pleased to meet you ...

Chinese leaders

Mao Zedong

Mao Zedong

Mao's parents were poor farmers. He only attended school until he was 13. Then he had to quit to work on the family farm. Mao was married four times and had 10 children.

He was a soldier in the Revolutionary Army and fought against the Qing Dynasty. In 1949, Mao founded the People's Republic of China. He became the Chairman of the Communist Party and the leader of China. He was able to unite the country, but **millions and millions of Chinese people lost their lives** under his hard and cruel regime.

14th Dalai Lama

The Dalai Lama is an important spiritual leader to those who practice the religion of Buddhism. The current Dalai Lama was born to a family that raised horses. He has seven brothers and sisters. As the Dalai Lama, he teaches peace, nonviolence, and kindness.

Buddhists believe in reincarnation, which means that when someone dies, their spirits are born again into a new body. After the 13th Dalai Lama died, religious leaders found a two-year-old boy who showed signs of being a reincarnation of the 13th Dalai Lama. So that boy became the 14th Dalai Lama.

14th Dalai Lama

Tell Leonardo what you think:

Do you think Mao Zedong was a good leader? Circle **YES** or **NO**

Is the Dalai Lama a nice man? Circle **YES** or **NO**

Did you know?

The Dalai Lama should live in the Potala Palace in Tibet, but he is living in exile in India because he and other Tibetans have a conflict with the Chinese government.

Not all famous people in China are leaders!

Bruce Lee

Bruce Lee

Born Lee Jun Fan, he was a child actor in the United States and Hong Kong. He starred in around 20 films as a child. As a young man, he became a famous action hero, starring in a US television show called *The Green Hornet*. He also became the star of other television shows and movies, and he taught martial arts classes.

Bruce moved back to Hong Kong in 1971 and made popular movies that broke box office records. He became a **major movie star all over Asia**.

Do you know a famous movie star from your country?

____

Li Na

Li Na is a famous tennis player who won many titles and awards. She started playing tennis when she was a little girl and became a professional.

She played on China's National Tennis Team, and studied tennis at the John Newcombe Academy in America. She is the second Chinese tennis player (after Zheng Jie) to defeat a world-record holder. Li retired from tennis after getting a lot of injuries.

Li Na

Do you know a famous sports star from your country?

____

Food in China:
five flavors and eight cuisines

Chinese food is popular just about everywhere in the world!

The Chinese describe food as having five flavors: sweet, sour, salty, bitter, and spicy. They divide the different foods from all over China into eight types. The eight cuisines (or kinds of cooking) include Cantonese, Sichuan, Hunan, and five others. If you grow up to be a chef, you may study China's food groupings to learn how to put together yummy flavors.

Rice

Wheat

Noodles

Did you know?
It's said that ice cream was invented in China around 200 BC! They made it by packing a mixture of milk and rice into the snow. Do you think they should have called it "rice cream?!"

Ginger root

Standard ingredients in Chinese cooking include rice, various types of noodles, and wheat—used to make breads, **jiaozi** (a type of Chinese dumpling), and **mantou** (a type of steamed buns).

Sesame oil

Seasonings are very important to Chinese food. They include ginger root, sesame oil, garlic, scallions, white pepper, Sichuan peppercorns, and more.

Soy sauce is very popular all over the world. It was invented in China, and it's made from fermented soy beans and wheat.

Soy sauce

Have you tried it?
Leonardo thinks it tastes good! Do you?

Famous Chinese dishes

Did you know?
In China it's not nice to use knives on the table during meals. All of these dishes are meant to be eaten with **chopsticks**.

It's fun to try new things!

Check the box if you have tasted one of these popular Chinese dishes.

Sweet and Sour

Originally from Hunan, this is a popular dish worldwide.

Peking Roasted Duck

A famous dish from Beijing. Crisp roasted duck in a sauce.

Mapo doufu

From Sichuan, this tofu dish is served in a spicy sauce.

Chow Mein

These stir-fried noodles are popular all through China and many parts of the world.

Gong Bao

Also called Kung Pao or Kung Po, this is a spicy chicken stir-fry dish from Sichuan.

Dumplings

Dough is wrapped around a variety of fillings, and then steamed or fried.

Eating Chinese food the Chinese way

What's for breakfast?

Chinese breakfasts may look very different from what you are used to.

Can you circle the meals you'd like to try?

Steamed buns

Noodles

Soybean milk and fried dough sticks

Rice dumplings

Pancakes with eggs

Mealtimes in China

Breakfast is usually from 7:00 a.m. to 8:00 a.m.

Lunch is between noon and 2:00 p.m.

Dinner is a very important meal in China. Dinner is between 6:00 p.m. and 8:00 p.m. Dinner includes soup, meats, vegetables, and rice. There may be lots of different courses.

Draw the hands on the clock to show Leonardo what time you like to eat breakfast!

Table Manners in China

- Don't take food from serving dishes with your chopsticks.
- Don't use your chopsticks to point at food or gesture while talking.
- Do slurp your noodles and soup! It's expected.
- Do cover your mouth when using a toothpick.

Using Chopsticks

Can you hold your chopsticks like this? 

Move the top chopstick with your thumb and forefinger to pinch food against the second chopstick.

Ordering Chinese food in China!

Here are some Chinese phrases you can practice to help you order food in a Chinese restaurant.

- 请 (*qǐng*)
  "**Please.**"
- 谢谢 (*xiè xiè!*)
  Thank you!
- 点菜! (*diǎn cài*)
  "**I would like to order.**"
- 一壶茶水! (*yī hú chá shuǐ*)
  One pot of tea!"
- 一份宫保鸡丁! (*yī fèn gōng bào jī dīng*)
  "**One serving of Kung Pao Chicken!**"

If your menu has pictures, you can point to the picture of the item you want and say:

一这个, 一份 (*zhè gè, yī fèn*)
"**One serving of this.**"

Did you know?
You may be used to being very polite to waiters in restaurants, but that is not how it is in China. Even in fancy restaurants, people yell, "**Waiter! Order food!**"

服务员! 点菜
(*fú wù yuán! diǎn cài!*)

You don't need to worry about hurting your waiter's feelings or offending them if you yell—**that's just the way it's done in China!**

Did you know?
Certain foods in China are very strange to outsiders. Some Chinese people enjoy eating **snakes**, **scorpions**, and **frogs**!

Practice saying "please"(*qǐng*) in Chinese.
It sounds a little bit like "SING."
How did you do?

Circle: **OK** **GOOD** **NOT SO GOOD**

Practice writing the Chinese characters for "**I would like to order.**" 点菜

The Chinese language

北京

Chinese is the official language of China. But there are over 3,000 different dialects* of Chinese being spoken across China!

Instead of letters, Chinese uses symbols called characters. Three thousand years ago, the characters were first written as pictures that represented different items. These pictures changed over time to become the Chinese characters used today.

*A dialect is a form of a language that's only spoken in a certain area. It has its own pronunciation and vocabulary.

Help Leonardo to draw Chinese symbols for *tree*, *fire*, *person*.

tree	fire	person
		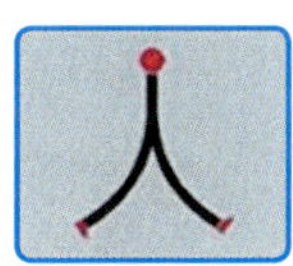

(mù)	*(huǒ)*	*(rén)*

Did you know?
More people are learning English in China than anywhere else in the world!

Did you know?
Writing of Chinese characters is an art called Chinese calligraphy. The characters are written in columns, from top to bottom and from right to left. If you were reading a book written in Chinese, you would start reading in the upper right corner of the page!

Chinese writing:
traditional and simplified

Chinese does not have an alphabet with letters. Students in ancient China had to memorize thousands of pictures and characters in order to learn to read and write!

Chinese characters continued to change even after **Emperor Qin**, first emperor of the **Qin Dynasty**, tried to standardize them.

The People's Republic of China, led by **Chairman Mao**, decided to make Chinese writing more simple in the 1950s. They created what's called Simplified Chinese.

Simplified Chinese characters use fewer strokes, and they are a bit easier to write than **Traditional Chinese**.

Here is the Simplified Chinese character for the phrase "to play" (*wán*).

玩

wán

Try to draw it in this box.

Traditional Chinese		Simplified Chinese
愛	love	爱
馬	horse	马
麵	noodle	面

Did you know?
There are over 40,000 Chinese characters! Children in school are expected to learn 5,000 characters. College graduates have usually memorized 10,000 or more.

Numbers in Chinese

If Chinese characters seem really difficult to write, Leonardo suggests you **try writing Chinese numbers**! They are pretty simple and fun to write.

Help Leonardo to draw Chinese numbers.

See if you can copy the Chinese character for each number in the box below it.

Did you know?
The number 8 is thought of as very lucky in China. That's why the 2008 Olympics in Beijing were scheduled to begin on 8/8/08 at 8:08:08 p.m.!

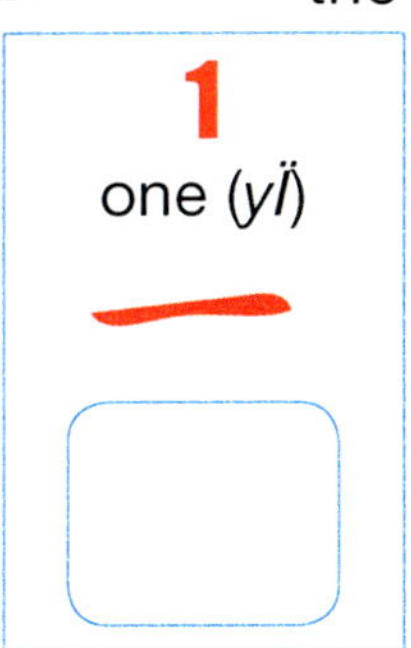

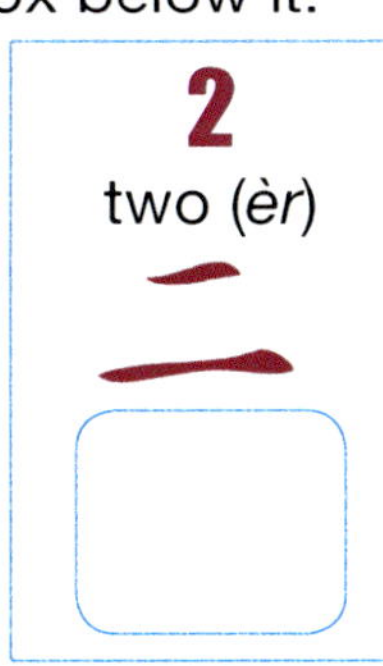

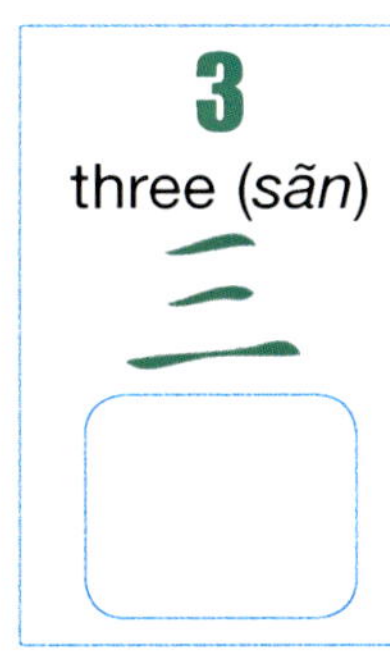

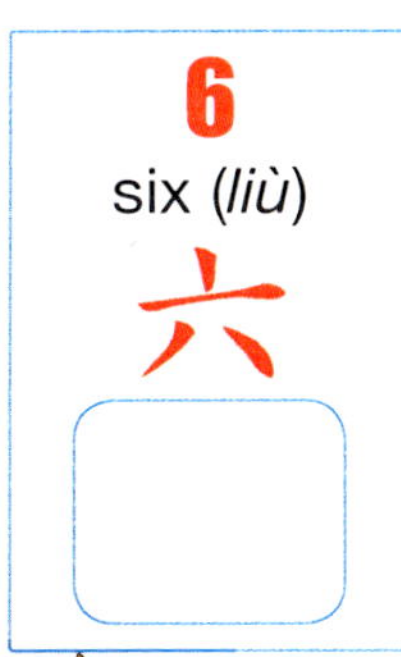

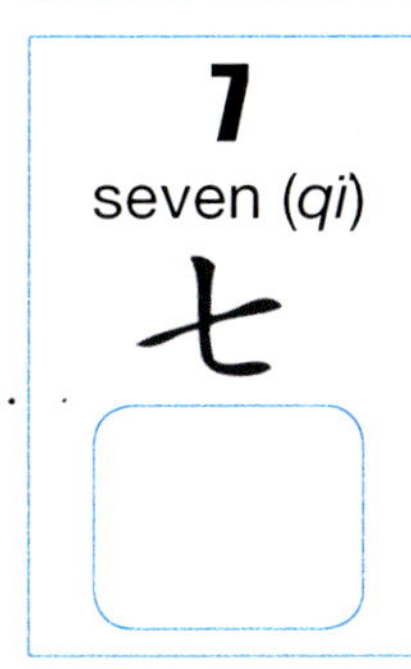

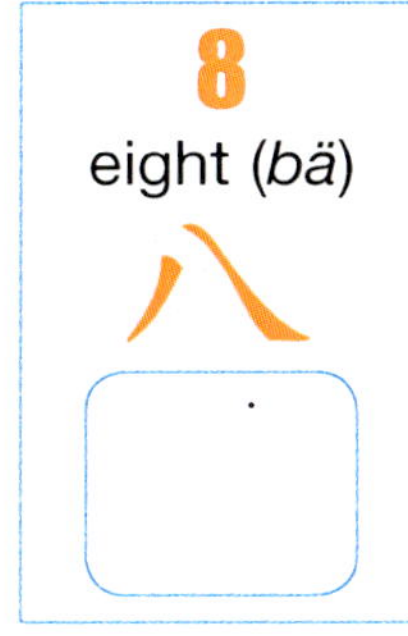

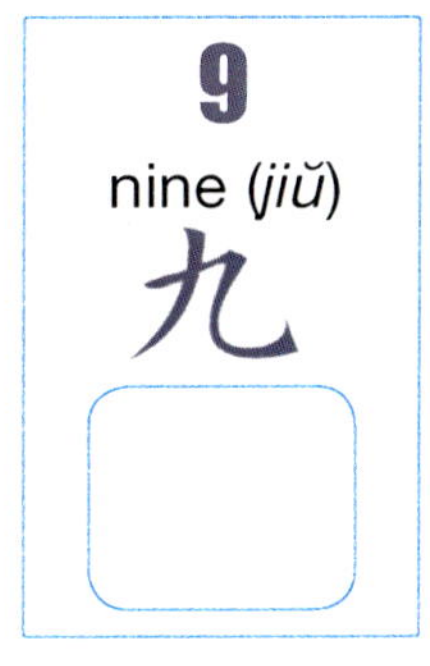

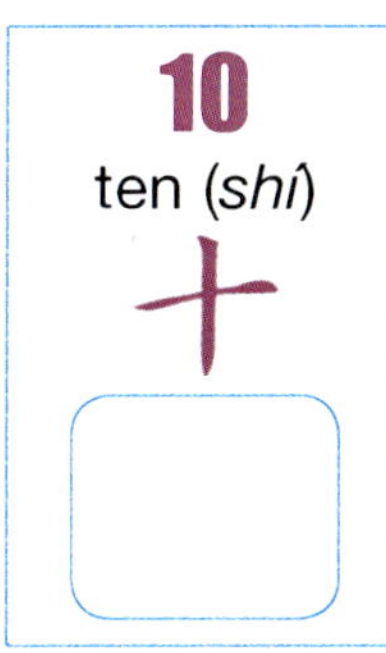

Your age in Chinese numbers:

The page number where you read about Buddha: ______________

Do you remember the **Five Dynasties**?
Write 5 in Chinese: ______________

Did you know?
The number 4 is considered very unlucky in China because the Chinese word for "four" sounds like the word for "death." Numbers 5 and 7 are unlucky as well.

Popular sports in China

Even in ancient times, sports were an important part of Chinese culture. Archaeologists have found signs that China had organized sports as far back as 4,000 years ago!

Today, the Chinese people are good at many different types of sports. Here are some of their favorites.

Bicycles

Chinese people love to ride bicycles. They ride them to work, for exercise, and for fun!

Martial Arts

Kung Fu is a famous fighting style that is now a traditional sport. There are different types of Kung Fu.

Basketball

China has been playing basketball almost as long as the United States and Canada. And their teams have won many awards.

Women's Volleyball

Volleyball is a very popular sport in China. The women's volleyball team has won many medals in the Olympics.

What is your favorite sport to play?

Fun Facts about China

- Dragons are considered to be very lucky and are positive symbols of power.
- Peking Duck is one of the most popular and favorite dishes in China.
- Many children keep crickets as pets in small cages made of wood.
- Over 80 percent of the world's toys are manufactured in China
- In addition to celebrating Mother's Day and Father's Day, China also celebrates a Children's Day.
- The Chinese invented kites to frighten enemies in battle.
- People who died while working on the Great Wall were buried beneath it.
- The Chinese invented suspension bridges in 25 BC. That was 1,800 years before European countries tried to build them.
- Chinese buildings rarely have a fourth floor because of their superstition about the number 4. In tall buildings, the floors will be numbered 1, 2, 3, 5 … and so on, skipping the number 4 altogether!
- Everyone in China has the same birthday. On the seventh day of the Chinese New Year, everyone turns a year older.
- There are more students in China than there are people in the entire country of Japan.
- Because boys are born more frequently than girls, and because the Chinese government only allowed each family to have one child for many years, there are 32 million more boys than girls in China.

What do you know about China?

1. Does China border the sea? Circle **YES** or **NO**.

2. What is the name of China's capital city? ______________

3. Can you remember what endangered animal lives in China? ______________

4. What color is China's flag? ______________ Does it have triangles on it? Circle **YES** or **NO**.

5. Circle **TRUE** or **FALSE**: Coins in ancient China used to be shaped like knives.

6. What is a dynasty? Choose the right answer:

   a) A type of crown with jewels.
   b) A period where one family rules.
   c) A tomb where emperors are buried.

7. Umbrellas were invented in China. Circle **TRUE** or **FALSE**.

8. What is China's biggest holiday? Choose the right answer:

   a) Christmas
   b) Chinese New Year
   c) The Lantern Festival

爱

9. Does Chinese writing use letters? Circle **YES** or **NO**.

10. The Dalai Lama was born in Tibet. Circle **TRUE** or **FALSE**.

11. Dumplings are a kind of Chinese food. Circle **TRUE** or **FALSE**.

Answers: 1. YES; 2. Beijing; 3. Giant panda; 4. Red / NO; 5. TRUE; 6. b); 7. TRUE; 8. b); 9. NO; 10. TRUE; 11. TRUE.

And to sum it all up ...

SUMMARY OF THE TRIP

We had great fun! What a pity it is over ...

Which places did we visit?

____

____

Whom did we meet ...

- Did you meet tourists from other countries? yes / no
  If you did meet tourists, where did they come from?
  (Name their nationalities):

____

Shopping and souvenirs ...

- What did you buy on the trip?

____

____

- What did you want to buy, but ended up not buying?

____

Experiences ...

- What are the most memorable experiences of the trip?

____

____

____

What was each family member's favorite place?

_______________ : ____________________________

_______________ : ____________________________

_______________ : ____________________________

_______________ : ____________________________

Grade the most beautiful places and the best experiences of your journey:

First place

Second place

Third place

And now, a difficult task—talk with your family and decide:

What did everyone enjoy most on the trip?

Date	What did we do?

SURPRISE YOUR KIDS
WITH LEONARDO'S PERSONAL GIFTS!

Every week Leonardo sends prizes (backpacks, posters, stickers, and more) to a few lucky children who read our books. New winners each week!

Just send your email address to enter your child in the drawing. PLUS—each child entered will immediately receive a free Kids' Travel Kit and a 25% off promo code for your next journey with FlyingKids®.

Leonardo wants to make your kids happy!
Sign up today at www.theflyingkids.com/happybuyers

ENJOY MORE FUN ADVENTURES WITH LEONARDO AND FlyingKids®

Find more Guides to many destinations at www.theflyingkids.com

Get lots of information about family travel, free activities, and special offers

FlyingKidsForYou

@FlyingKidsForYou

@TheFlyingKids1

Made in United States
North Haven, CT
05 February 2025